BIBLE KEY WORDS

XII. HOPE

BIBLE KEY WORDS
FROM GERHARD KITTEL'S
*THEOLOGISCHES WÖRTERBUCH
ZUM NEUEN TESTAMENT*

HOPE

BY

RUDOLF BULTMANN

and KARL HEINRICH RENGSTORF

ADAM & CHARLES BLACK
LONDON

FIRST PUBLISHED 1963
A. AND C. BLACK LIMITED
4, 5 AND 6 SOHO SQUARE, LONDON W.1

Translation from the German
by Dorothea M. Barton, M.A.
edited by P. R. Ackroyd, Ph.D.

PRINTED IN GREAT BRITAIN BY
ROBERT CUNNINGHAM AND SONS LTD, ALVA

EDITOR'S PREFACE

THIS book is a translation of the article 'Eλπίς, written by Professors Rudolf Bultmann and Karl Heinrich Rengstorf in the *Theologisches Wörterbuch zum Neuen Testament* (TWNT), begun by G. Kittel and now edited by G. Friedrich, Vol. II, pp. 515-31. Apart from some curtailing of footnotes, the whole text of this short article is here translated and follows the order of the original. At the beginning of Chapter II a short addition has been made in the form of a list of the Hebrew words used in the Old Testament, to provide the basic information for the discussion which then follows.

The book traces the Greek usage of ἐλπίς with its predominantly neutral sense of 'expectation', and shows how it then does duty for the Old Testament terms in which anticipation of good or evil make for a feeling of hope or anxiety. Considerable space is devoted to the study of the development of the Messianic hope and to Rabbinic ideas, alongside those of the early church in which hope in God is in the Pauline literature a particularly important concomitant of faith. It is this Godward direction of hope—both in the Old Testament and in the New—which marks it off from any mere forethought or calculation of the future. In Chapter III the discussion of the Rabbinic material leads to the problem of the assurance of salvation, a problem which must be a pressing one in any religion which lays stress upon human obedience. That the problem is one with which Christians are concerned too is clear from the great deal of discussion which there has been at various times about assurance. The Christian's assurance rests

in God and not in himself. But this means that it is not
susceptible of exact demonstration, and that there must
always remain in Christian thinking an element of the
kind of agnosticism which recognises that it is improper
so to reckon upon God's saving power as to make of
Him less than He is—a means to an end.

The publication of the volume means that the triad
Faith, *Hope* and *Love* is now complete. Cross-reference
to the other two volumes has been made at one or two
obvious points, but it is clear that the three concepts
belong so closely together in Christian thinking that the
discussion of any one of them must inevitably evoke the
others, and the reader will frequently observe how
nearly the terms overlap within the richness of New
Testament thought.

All Hebrew words have been transliterated and,
where necessary, translated. Greek words are not transliterated. Where quotations are given from elsewhere
than the New Testament (or Septuagint), a translation
has been given, except where the meaning is evident or
where the actual Greek word used is of particular importance. In a number of cases translations have been
given of crucial Greek words, but these are to be taken
only as rough guides to the meaning, since, as will
appear from their contents, these are words which are
deserving of full and separate study. Such of them as
appear in the New Testament are, of course, so treated
in other volumes of TWNT.

Biblical references follow the normal chapter and verse
enumeration of the Hebrew and Greek texts, with a note
of deviations in the English versions. References to the
Septuagint therefore in some cases require modification,
particularly in the Psalter and in the book of Jeremiah.

CONTENTS

BIBLIOGRAPHY

STOBAEUS: *Eclogae* IV.997-1007.

TH. BIRT: *Elpides* (1881).

L. SCHMIDT: *Die Ethik der alten Griechen*, II (1882), pp. 69-74.

H. DE GUIBERT: *Recherches de Science Religieuse*, 4 (1913), pp. 565-596.

A. POTT: *Das Hoffen im NT* (1915).

F. WEHRLI: *ΛΑΘΕ ΒΙΩΣΑΣ* (1931), pp. 6 ff.

A. LESKI: *Gnomon*, 9 (1933), pp. 173 ff.

CHAPTER III

H. L. STRACK and P. BILLERBECK: *Kommentar zum NT aus Talmud und Midrasch*, I-V (²1956), see III, pp. 217 ff.

Jewish Encyclopaedia, VI, pp. 459 f.

G. F. MOORE: *Judaism*, I-III (1927-30), see II, pp. 287 ff.

W. BOUSSET: *Die Religion des Judentums im späthellenistischen Zeitalter*, ed. by H. Gressmann (³1926), see index under 'Hoffnung'.

G. KITTEL: *Die Religionsgeschichte und das Urchristentum* (1932), pp. 130 ff.

E. STAUFFER: 'Paulus und Akiba. Der erlösende und der tragische Ausgang des Judentums', *Saat auf Hoffnung*, 69 (1932), pp. 113 ff.

W. WICHMANN: *Die Leidenstheologie* (1930).

S. MOWINCKEL: *He that cometh* (ET 1956).

Reference may also be made to the general theologies of the Old and New Testaments, and to A. Richardson, ed., *A Theological Word Book of the Bible* (1950), and J.-J. von Allmen, *Vocabulary of the Bible* (1958).

ABBREVIATIONS

Anth Pal	*Anthologia Palatina*, ed. Stadtmüller and Bucherer (1906).
BMI	*Collection of Ancient Greek Inscriptions in the British Museum* (1874 ff.).
Diels	H. Diels, *Die Fragmente der Vorsokratiker*, ed. W. Kranz (I, ⁷1954; II, III, ⁶1952); cf. K. Freeman, *Ancilla to the PreSocratic Philosophers. A complete translation of the fragments in Diels* . . . (1948).
Ditt Or	W. Dittenberger, *Orientis Graeci Inscriptiones Selectae*, I-II (1903-5).
Ditt Syll	W. Dittenberger, *Sylloge Inscriptionum Graecarum*, I-IV, 1, 2 (³1915-24).
Epigr Graec	*Epigrammata Graeca ex lapidis conlecta*, ed. Kaibel (1878).
ET	English translation.
EVV	English versions.
Pr-Bauer	E. Preuschen, *Griechisch-deutsches Wörterbuch* . . . *NT*, ed. W. Bauer (⁵1958). ET of ed. 4 (1949 ff.) by W. F. Arndt and F. W. Gingrich (1957).
Str-B	Strack-Billerbeck, cf. Bibliography.
Thes Steph	H. Stephanus, *Thesaurus Graecae Linguae* (1831 ff.).
TWNT	*Theologisches Wörterbuch zum Neuen Testament*, ed. G. Friedrich.

I. THE GREEK CONCEPT OF HOPE

1. *General usage.*

'*We are always filled with hopes all our lives.*' These words from Plato's *Philebus* 39e occur in an analysis in which he demonstrates how human existence is determined not only by the αἴσθησις (perception) which apprehends the present, but also by the μνήμη (memory) of the past and the expectation of what is to come[1]; in fact what happens is that both the remembrance of the past and the expectation of what is to come (προχαίρειν and προλυπεῖσθαι, 39d) are not based on objective judgement and calculation, but on an expectation for oneself, a fear or a hope, the content of which in each case grows out of what a man understands to be possible for himself. 'What a man is determines what he hopes and how he hopes.'[2] He whose hopes are real (ἀληθεῖς) is favoured by the gods (θεοφιλής). Expectations and hopes are the images which a man forms for himself of his future.

It is an attribute of human nature to have ἐλπίδες,[3] that is to say, to begin with: expectations of the future (ἐλπίς = προσδοκία[4]), happy ones and sad ones. What

---

[1] Ἐλπίς and μνήμη have a similar relationship in Aristot. *Metaph.* XI.7, p. 1072b, 18; *Rhet.* II.8, p. 1386a, 2 f., 30; *De Memoria* I, p. 449b, 10 ff.

[2] H. G. Gadamer, *Platos dialektische Ethik* (1931), p. 138; cf. the whole of his interpretation of *Philebus* 35a-41b on pp. 126-39.

[3] Stob. V.1001.13 f.; Eur. *Tro.* 632 f.; he who loves, hopes; Plat. *Phileb.* 39e; Theocr. 4.42; cf. Birt, *op. cit.*, pp. 6 ff.

[4] The examples in note 1 above show this; cf. Plat. *Phileb.* 36a ff.; ἐλπίς = anxious expectation, apprehension, e.g. Eur. *Iph. Aul.* 786. Ἐλπίζειν often means to believe, to suppose, e.g. Pind. fr. 61;

we mean by hope is called ἐλπὶς ἀγαθή,[1] even though later on ἐλπίς by itself is used with the meaning of hope,[2] in which the original etymological sense of the stem ἐλπ- is again brought out.[3]

But the manner in which the fact that ἐλπίζειν is a component part of man's nature is interpreted on each occasion, is very significant for the Greek understanding of human existence. In Soph. *Ant.* 615 f. the equivocal value of ἐλπίς is expressed:

> *To many hope may come in wanderings wild, a solace and a joy*
> *To many, shows of fickle-hearted love.*

Emped. fr. 11 (I.227.21 Diels); Heracl. fr. 27 (I.83.5 f. Diels); Aristoph. *Av.* 956. Παρ' ἐλπίδα is often used as a synonym for παρὰ γνώμην (cf. TWNT I, p. 690, n. 7) cf. Soph. *Ant.* 330 f. Ἀνέλπιστος = 'unexpected', e.g. Eur. *Iph. Taur.* 1495; *Hel.* 412. Synonymous with ἀδόκητος, *Hel.* 656.

[1] Plat. *Leg.* I.644e. The nature of ἐλπίς is determined by attributes such as ἀγαθή (Pind. *Isthm.* 8.15; Plat. *Leg.* IV.718a; Aristot. *De Virtutibus et Vitiis* 8, p. 1251b, 34 f.; Ael. Arist. *Or. Sacr.* 48.28); καλή (Plut. *De Bruto* 40 [I.1002c]; Stob. I.403.21); γλυκεῖα (Pind. fr. 214; Plat. *Resp.* I.331a); ἱλαρά (Critias fr. 6 [II.315.11 Diels]); χρηστή (BMI 894, in P. Wendland, *Die hellenistisch-römische Kultur* [1912], p. 410; often in Philo); on the other hand as κακή (Plat. *Resp.* I.330a). Frequently the adjective εὔελπις (Plat. *Ap.* 41d; *Phaed.* 64a): to be εὔελπις is a typical quality of youth, in Aristot. *Rhet.* II.12, p. 1389a, 19 ff. The leading character in Aristoph. *Av.* is Εὐελπίδης 'Hope well'.

[2] Thus in Pseud.-Plat. *Def.* 418a ἐλπίς is defined as προσδοκία ἀγαθοῦ. This usage agrees with the contrast frequently made later between ἐλπίς and φόβος, Birt, *op. cit.*, pp. 6 (and p. 97, n. 17), 46 f. —Later ἐλπίς (ἐλπίζειν) is occasionally used beside προσδοκία (προσδοκᾶν), see Preisigke, *Wörterbuch der griech. Papyrusurkunden* (1925 ff.).

[3] Ελπ-: an extension of the root *vel* (Latin *vel-le*) with *p*: as in Latin also in *volup* (*voluptas*); in Greek ἀλπ- in ἔπαλπνος 'desirable', ἀλπαλέος, ἁρπαλέος, ἄλπιστος, cf. A. Walde–J. Pokorny, *Vergleichendes Wörterbuch der indo-germanischen Sprachen* I (1930), p. 295.

It is a solace for man in the midst of present troubles that, or if, he may still hope, cf. Hom. *Od.* 16.101 and 19.84: *for there is yet room for hope.* Hope is 'golden' (Soph. *Oed. Tyr.* 158) and the soul is disheartened which lacks its accustomed confidence of hope (Aesch. *Ag.* 994; cf. 262).

Pind. fr. 214: *Sweet companion with him, to cheer his heart and nurse his old age, accompanieth Hope, who chiefly ruleth the changeful mind of mortals.*[1]

Pind. *Isthm.* 8.15: *It is meet for man to take to heart good hope.*[2]

According to Thuc. V.103 ἐλπίς is an abating of danger. It can comfort the individual when in distress (in Democr. fr. 287 [II.20.5 f. in Diels]). Hence the old fable[3] which tells how Zeus gave man a cask filled with all good things, but that man beguiled by curiosity

---

[1] Plato in *Resp.* I.331a quotes this verse with the remark: *But him who is conscious of no wrong that he has done a sweet hope ever attends and a goodly . . .* , whilst the wicked lives *with an evil hope*; cf. *Leg.* IV.718a concerning the upright man: Aristot. *De Virtutibus et Vitiis* 8, p. 1251b, 33 f.; Eur. *Hel.* 1031. Cf. the opposite in Democr. fr. 221 (II.105.10 f. in Diels). Thus in Hesiod *Op.* 498 ff. ἐλπίς tempts the work-shy man to make bad plans.

[2] cf. Soph. *Trach.* 25 f.; Eur. *Herc. Fur.* 105 f.

[3] The original meaning of the fable is obviously preserved in Babrius 58 (P. Friedländer, *Herakles* [1907], pp. 39 ff.); in Hes. *Op.* 94 ff. it is elaborated, but the meaning is disputed (H. Türck, *Pandora und Eva* [1931], pp. 15 ff.). The same idea occurs in Theognis 1135 f. although he is aware that hope is double edged. In later times cf. Max. Tyr. 29, 6 b/c. In Heracl. fr. 18 (I.81.16 f. in Diels) ἐλπίς seems to be considered as the suprarational power in invention. According to H. Fränkel (in Türck, *op. cit.*, p. 6) contrary to Diels: 'He who does not expect what is not to be expected (that which exceeds all expectations) will not discover what is undiscoverable (inconceivable) and inaccessible.' For the significance of ἐλπίς as the motive force of craftsmanship which leads to prosperity see Birt, *loc. cit.*

lifted the lid, so that all the good things escaped to the gods, and as the lid was slammed down ἐλπίς alone still remained captive and now consoles mankind. The same theme occurs in Aesch. *Prom.* 248 ff.; Prometheus boasts: *I caused mortals no longer to foresee their doom* and in reply to the question: *Of what sort was the cure thou didst find for this affliction?* he answers: *I caused blind hopes to dwell within their breasts.* Whereupon the chorus says: *A great boon was this thou gavest to mortals.*

But hope is easily led astray[1] and is dangerous. Only a god is not mistaken in his expectations,[2] the ἐλπίδες of man are unreliable.[3] Man must not aspire to the distant but to the familiar, he must seize what is at his feet.[4] 'Ελπίς which waits for what is uncertain is contrasted with modesty of forethought (Pind. *Olymp.* 7.44). By means of forethought (Pind. *Nem.* 11.46) man makes himself master of the future by basing his judgement on present circumstances and acting accordingly. Thucydides (II.62) contrasts *hope which is strongest in perplexity* with *reason, supported by the facts, which gives a surer insight*

[1] cf. Plat. *Tim.* 69d. The (θεὸς) ἐλπίς leads astray in Eur. *Iph. Taur.* 414 ff.; *Suppl.* 479 ff.

[2] Pind. *Pyth.* 2.49.

[3] Pind. *Olymp.* 12.5 f. (in general: 12.1-13 and *Pyth.* 10.59-64, 12.28-32); *Pyth.* 3.19-23. In *Nem.* 11.42-48 destiny directs the race of mortals, but our limbs are fettered by unfortunate hope; this wells up out of ἔρως, *desire* (cf. for this *Pyth.* 10.60; *Nem.* 3.30; Soph. *Ant.* 616; Plat. *Symp.* 193a). In *Isthm.* 2.43 the envious hopes hang round the souls of mortals. Cf. Solon fr. i.35 f. (Diehl). A hope is rarely fulfilled: Aesch. *Ag.* 505. Cf. Soph. fr. 205. In Soph. *Aj.* 477; cf. also e.g. Hes. *Op.* 498; M. Ant. 3.14; *Anth. Pal.* VII.376; for the opposite see πιστὸν ἔλπισμα in Epic. fr. 68 (Usener) (for this Plut. *Suav. Viv. Epic.* 6 [II.1090d]: πιστὴ ἐλπίς). Antiphon fr. 38 (II.303.2 f. Diels). For the relationship between hopes and dreams Birt, *op. cit.*, pp. 45 ff.

[4] Pind. *Pyth.* 3.20, 22, 60, 10.63; *Isthm.* 8.18.

into the future. This corresponds to the contrast in II.42 between ἐλπίς and ἔργον. In V.103 man goes astray if he takes refuge from his uncertain hopes in divination and the oracles.[1] According to Democritus the ἐλπίδες of fools cannot be realised; those of reasonable and educated men are better than the wealth of the uneducated (fr. 58 [II.120.20 f. Diels]); for the ἐλπίς of the clever man, which in that case is in fact no longer ἐλπίς in its original sense, is based not on τύχη (luck) but on φύσις (nature) which can be investigated scientifically.[2] The peculiarly Greek propensity to safeguard oneself against the future by intelligent adaptation to the order of the cosmos is expressed here in a characteristic way.

2. *Plato*

Plato indeed does not need to cut out ἔρως working effectively in ἐλπίς (cf. p. 4, n. 3), since he considers it to be the driving force towards the beautiful and the good. Therefore he can say of it in *Symp.* 193d: *Not only in the present does he (ἔρως) bestow the priceless boon of bringing us to our very own, but he also supplies this excellent hope for the future.* For Plato himself these *hopes for the future* already transcend the life of this world. When the darkness hides from man another better life, so that we being infatuated cling to the dubious glamour of earthly life (Eur. *Hipp.* 189 ff.), the philosopher is εὔελπις in face of death (Plat. *Ap.* 41c, *Phaed.* 64a). For he cherishes πολλὴ ἐλπίς that he will gain there *fully that which has been my chief object in my past life* (*Phaed.* 67b), and he

---

[1] cf. Aristot. *De Memoria* 1, p. 449b, 10 ff.

[2] cf. fr. 176 (II.96.12 ff. Diels). Cf. the contrary view in Heracl. (cf. p. 3, n. 3).

does not fear death (*Phaed.* 67c-68b), *for the prize is fair
and the hope great* (114c). After all many have already
even died of their own free will, supported by the hope
that they will see again those of their own family who
have preceded them in death (*Phaed.* 68a).[1] The mysteries which promise to their initiates a blessed life after
their death[2] acquire increasing importance. Belief in the
mysteries is also the reason why in Porphyry *Marc.* 24
ἐλπίς is reckoned with πίστις, ἀλήθεια and ἔρως as one
of the four elements (στοιχεῖα) which make up real life[3];
however the desire and hope for ephemeral things must
of course be cast aside (*op. cit.*, 29).[4]

3. *Hellenistic usage*

Of course earthly and human hopes also play their
part in Hellenism beside hopes for the future.[5] Just as
the gift of Zeus to mankind consists in his control of war
and his bestowal of τύχη, ἐλπίς and εἰρήνη,[6] so too
Augustus in the Priene Inscription is praised as the
saviour who brings war to an end, fulfils old hopes and
arouses fresh ones.[7] Stoicism devoted no attention to

[1] cf. *Life and Death*, to be published in this series.

[2] Isoc. 4.28, 8.34; Ael. Arist. 22.10. Cic. *De Legibus* II.14.36,
*we have gained the power not only to live happily but also to die with a
better hope.*—Cf. C. A. Lobeck, *Aglaophamus* (1829), pp. 69 ff.;
E. Rohde, *Psyche* I (ed. 10, 1925), p. 290.

[3] The literature given in *Love* in this series, p. 59, n. 4. Porphyry
describes in *op. cit.* how life is determined by the four elements.
Cf. in addition Plut. *De Bruto* 40 (I.1002c).

[4] cf. in addition Jul. *Ep.* 89, p. 124.13, 139.2 f.

[5] For the role of ἐλπίς in the erotic literature see Birt, *op. cit.*, 3 f.;
in the comedies and the Hellenistic and Latin literature influenced
by it see Birt, *passim*; as an example especially Luc. *De Mercede
Conductis.* Cf. also *Anth. Pal.* VI.330.1 f.; P. Oxy. VII.1070.10 f.

[6] cf. Stob. I 393.19 ff., 403.21.

[7] Ditt Or II.458 (in Wendland, *op. cit.*, pp. 409 f.). Similarly

the phenomenon of hope. In Epictetus ἐλπίζειν (ἐλπίς) is used with its early meaning of expecting.[1] He knows: *We ought to measure both the length of our stride, and the extent of our hope, by what is possible* (fr. 31); he emphasises: *We ought neither to fasten our ship to one small anchor nor our life to a single hope* (fr. 30); he exhorts, not *to look to others*, but *to hope from yourself* (III.26.11). Similarly Marc. Aur. Ant. exhorts: *Casting away all empty hopes, come to thine own rescue* (3.14).[2] The sentence of Epicurus is characteristic: *We must remember that the future is neither wholly ours nor wholly not ours, so that neither must we count upon it as quite certain to come nor despair of it as quite certain not to come* (Diog. L.X.127). In the *Anth. Pal.* IX.172.1: *neither hope nor good luck concerns me*.[3] Here it is taken for granted everywhere that ἐλπίς contains the image of a future devised from man himself.

in the inscription of Halicarnassus BMI 894 (cf. p. 2, n. 1); Ditt Syll[3] 797.5 f.; Ditt Or 542.12, 669.7: ἐλπίζειν in the emperor (Galba); P. Oxy. VII.1021.5 ff. Cf. the inscription from Tomi lines 3 f., 34 f. published in the *Archaeol.-epigr. Mitteilungen* 14 (1891), pp. 22-26.

[1] I.20.13; II.20.37, 23.46; *Ench.* 40.

[2] cf. in addition for ἐλπίζειν 9.29, 10.36; for ἐλπίς 1.17, 5.8.

[3] Frequently ἐλπίς and τύχη are linked together, Birt, *op. cit.*, pp. 15 (p. 100, n. 57), 47, 91 (and 125, n. 215). *Spes et fortuna, valete*, is found in a Roman epigram on a tomb-stone. *Carmina Latina Epigraphica* (ed. Buecheler), 409.8.

II. THE CONCEPT OF HOPE IN THE OLD TESTAMENT

1. *Hebrew vocabulary and Septuagint renderings*

The OT uses the following words for *hope*: The commonest is the root *bāṭaḥ* (more than 100 times) and its derivatives *mibṭaḥ* (15), *beṭaḥ* (43), and also *biṭṭāḥōn*. The idea of *trust, security* is the most obvious here. Three other roots occur about 40 times each—*qāwāh, to wait* —and its derivative *tiqwāh, hope* (32); *ḥāsāh, to seek refuge*—and its derivative *maḥseh, refuge* (20); *yāḥal* (in pi'el and hiph'il, *to wait*—and its derivative *tōḥelet, hope* (6). Other words which occur seldom are: *sābar* (pi'el), *to hope, wait* (6); *sēber, hope*; *kesel, kislah, confidence* (5). The translations given here are only approximate and reference should be made to the discussion which follows.

The LXX as a rule renders *bāṭaḥ* and the nouns derived from it with ἐλπίζειν (ἐλπίς)[1]; yet for this group of words πεποιθέναι (πεποίθησις) often occurs. But πιστεύειν is never used. In addition, ἐλπίζειν stands twice for *qāwāh*, which is mostly rendered by ὑπομένειν (also ἀνα- and περι-), whilst ἐλπίς appears mainly for *tiqwāh* (only in Proverbs and Job and in addition in Ezek. xxxvii.11); πεποιθέναι (Isa. viii.17, xxxiii.2), προσδοκᾶν, ἐγγίζειν, ἐπέχειν are also used for *qāwāh*, ὑπόστασις and ὑπομονή for *tiqwāh*.

[1] Ἐλπίζειν occurs 47 times for *bāṭaḥ*, once for *beṭaḥ* (?); ἐλπίς too occurs 7 times for *bāṭaḥ*. In addition ἐλπίς is found 9 times for *mibṭaḥ*, 14 times for *beṭaḥ*, once for *biṭṭāḥōn*. On the breathing of ἐλπίς (ἐλπίζειν) see Thackeray, pp. 124 f.

Ἐλπίζειν is put 20 times for ḥāsāh and 7 times for maḥseh; yet πεποιθέναι also stands 9 times for ḥāsāh and σκέπη, καταφυγή, βοηθός for maḥseh. The pi'el of yāḥal is rendered 10 times and its hiph'il 5 times by ἐλπίζειν; here too ὑπομένειν occurs beside it. Tōḥelet appears twice as ἐλπίς, once as ὑπόστασις, elsewhere other periphrases are met with.

Lastly sābar is rendered twice by ἐλπίζειν (twice by προσδοκᾶν); ἐλπίς is used once for sēber (so is προσδοκία once), once for kesel, once in a variant reading for mabbāṭ (Zech. ix.5 AQ). In addition there are odd cases: ἐλπίζειν for dārash (Isa. xi.10), gālal (Ps. xxii.9 [EVV 8, LXX xxi.9]), ḥashaq (Ps. xci.14 [LXX xc.14]), shā'an (II Chron. xiii.18), shāqaq (Isa. xxix.8), rᵉḥaṣ (Dan. iii.28), nāsā' nephesh (Jer. xliv.14) etc.; ἐλπίς for ḥāzūt (Isa. xxviii.18), ḥesed (II Chron. xxxv.26), ṣᵉbī (Isa. xxiv.16, xxviii.4 f.) nāsā' nephesh (Deut. xxiv.15); ἐλπὶς πονηρά for zᵉwā'āh (Isa. xxviii.19).

2. Old Testament usage

These facts are characteristic; they show that for the OT there is no neutral concept of ἐλπίς, which merely denotes expecting, so that an expectation would have to be qualified by the addition of good or bad as a hope or a fear. On the contrary to hope and to fear (with the future in view) are differentiated in the language from the first.[1] To hope, as the expectation of what is good, is closely connected with confidence, and the expectation means at the same time being eagerly on the look-out, in which the idea of patient waiting as well as that of seeking refuge may be emphasised.

[1] It is significant that where ἐλπὶς πονηρά occurs in the LXX (Isa. xxviii.19) it is a rendering of zᵉwā'āh, terror, horror.

Thus hope is always hoping for something good, and as long as a man lives, he hopes (Eccles. ix.4). But neither is such hope considered as a comforting fancy of the imagination, which may be forgotten in the distress of the present, nor is it a warning given against its uncertainty, as in the Greek world. On the contrary it is simply on hope that the life of the godly is fixed. To have hope and to have a future are an indication that a man is in a state of well-being.[1] Of course it is hope fixed on God.[2] Naturally this hope is primarily and normally expressed when a man finds himself in a distressing situation, out of which he hopes to be delivered and helped by God, and this hope is at the same time trust, so that *qāwāh* and *bāṭaḥ* appear side by side (Ps. xxv.1 ff.), or *qāwāh* occurs where otherwise *bāṭaḥ* is used in the same sense.[3] But this hopeful trust in God is

[1] Prov. xxiii.18, xxiv.14, xxvi.12; Job xi.18. If hope fails, then all is over, Lam. iii.18; Job vi.11, vii.6 *et passim*; the same is true of death, Isa. xxxviii.18; Ezek. xxxvii.4; Job xvii.15.

[2] He who trusts in God will receive help (Ps. xxvii.7), *will not be put to shame* (cf. TWNT I, p. 189, Ps. xxv.2 f., xxxi.6, 14, lxix.6, cxix.116; Isa. xlix.23). The fathers trusted in him and were not put to shame (Ps. xxii.4 f.). The godly trusts in God's *ḥesed* (Ps. xiii.5, xxxiii.18, 22, lii.9), *salvation* (*yeshū'āh*, Gen xlix.18; Ps. lxxviii.22), or *teshū'āh* (Ps. cxix.81, 123 *et passim*); he waits upon God (Ps. xxv.21) and upon his judgement (Isa. xxvi.8); God is his refuge (Ps. ix.19 [EVV 18], lxv.5, lxxi.5, xci.9 [EVV 8] *et passim*). Blessed is the man who trusts in God (Jer. xvii.7; Ps. xl.5 [EVV 4], xci.1 ff.). The godly ought to trust in God and wait upon him (Ps. i.5, xxvii.14, xxxviii.3 *et passim*; Prov. xx.22, xxii.19 *et passim*); he confesses: I trust (trusted) in God (Isa. xii.2; Ps. xxv.2, xxviii.7, xxxi.7, 15 [EVV 6, 14], xci.2).

[3] *Qāwāh* in Isa. viii.17, xxv.9, xxvi.8; Ps. xxvii.14, xxxvii.9, lxix.7 (EVV 6) *et passim*. *Bāṭaḥ* in Isa. xxx.15; Ps. xiii.6 (EVV 5), xxii.5 f. (EVV 4 f.) *et passim*. Similarly *ḥāsāh* (Ps. v.12 [EVV 11], xvii.7), where otherwise *qāwāh* occurs (Isa. xl.31; Ps. xxxvii.9, lxix.7 [EVV 6]; Lam. iii.25); *maḥseh* (Isa. xxviii.15; Ps. xiv.6,

demanded in every situation,[1] in the time of salvation as well.[2] Particularly when we reflect that the Psalms became the prayerbook of the community, it is clear that hopeful trust in God is demanded absolutely. The godly man knows that he always depends on what God will do, so that hope does not always expect something definite, does not fashion for itself a particular picture of the future, but consists in a quite general trust in God's protection and help.[3] Hence it can also be said that God is the hope, the confidence of the godly.[4] But in that case the Greek usage which contrasts ἐλπίς with what is at hand, with the familiar, or with foresight, anticipation on the basis of the available facts, is made impossible. The present too, which is thought by man to be at his disposal, is uncertain and cannot be turned to account. The distinction between hope and confi-

---

lxi.4 [EVV 3] *et passim*), where otherwise *mibṭaḥ* appears (Ps. xl.5 [EVV 4], lxv.6 [EVV 5]); in Ps. lxxi.5 *tiqwāh* and *mibṭaḥ* occur together; *maḥseh* follows in verse 7. In Jer. xvii.7 πεποιθέναι and ἐλπίζειν are both used as the rendering of *bāṭaḥ* and as that of *ḥāsāh* in Ps. lvii.2 (EVV 1); similarly in Isa. xxv.9 ἐλπίζειν and ὑπομένειν appear side by side for *qāwāh*.

[1] Jer. xvii.7; Ps. xl.5 (EVV 4), lii.9 (EVV 8), xci.2, cxii.7 *et passim*. [2] Isa. xii.2.

[3] This is brought out with particular emphasis where it is said that God grants hope instead of help (Jer. xxix.11, xxxi.17; Hos. ii.17 [EVV 15]); similarly when the time of salvation is described as a time of confidence (Isa. xxxii.18; Ezek. xxviii.26, xxxiv.27 f.). But this is also expressed by the fact that in the statements concerning hope much less is said about what is hoped for than about the reason for hoping (God, God's faithfulness, God's name and the like). So ἐλπίζειν (ἐλπίς) ἐπί with the dative or accusative, εἰς, ἐν, which are uncommon or rare forms of expression in Greek, become frequent in the LXX. In Greek ἐλπίζειν with the dative means 'to rely on' (Thuc. III.97.2); ἐλπίδες εἰς occurs in Thuc. III.14.1.

[4] Jer. xvii.7; Ps. lxi.4 (EVV 3), lxxi.5.

dence disappears, i.e. confidence and certainty are always at the same time a hope that the present situation will remain such that the factors on which one relies will endure in the future. But when this hope is not a hope in God, then all trust is an irresponsible assurance which God will fearfully disrupt and turn into dread and horror.[1] No one should trust in his riches (Ps. lii.9 [EVV 7]; Job xxxi.24), in his righteousness (Ezek. xxxiii.13), in men (Jer. xvii.5), in his religious possessions, whether it be the temple (Jer. vii.4) or Bethel (Jer. xlviii.13) or idols (Hab. ii.18). Men's deliberations and calculations are a breath (Ps. xciv.11); God brings them to nought (Ps. xxxiii.10; Isa. xix.3 etc.); *a man's mind plans his way, but the Lord directs his steps* (Prov. xvi.9). The people and its calculating politicians are put to shame when they build on the resources of force at their disposal and on treaties with foreign powers.[2] All such confidence imagines that it can rely on what is at its command, but hope should simply turn to Him who is not merely at one's disposal. Such trustful hope in God is delivered from fear (Isa. vii.4, xii.2; Ps. xlvi.3 [EVV 2]; Prov. xxviii.1); but it must continue strictly hand in hand with the fear of God (Isa. xxxii.11; Ps. xxxiii.18, xl.4 [EVV 3]; Prov. xiv.16, 26, xxiii.17). Therefore a man must be still and wait upon God.[3] The antithesis is seen in Job who refuses to wait (Job vi.11, xiii.15; cf. II Kings vi.33).

[1] Amos vi.1; Isa. xxxii.9-11; Zeph. ii.15; Prov. xiv.16. 'Carefree' in a neutral sense, without any criticism expressed, in Judg. xviii.7, 10, 27; Jer. xii.5; Job xl.23 (of the hippopotamus).

[2] Hos. x.13; Isa. xxxi.1; II Kings xviii.24; Isa. xxxvi.6, 9; Jer. ii.37; Ezek. xxix.16.

[3] Isa. xxx.15; Ps. xxxvii.5-7, where *quietness*, or *being still* and *waiting patiently* are combined with *bāṭaḥ* etc.

Whilst at first God's help is expected to relieve actual trouble,[1] it is considered more and more to be the eschatological help which brings all troubles to an end.[2] The attitude of confident waiting and trustful hope develops more and more into the awareness that all earthly things and those of the present time are entirely temporary, and becomes the hope for the eschatological future.

[1] Ps. xiii.6, xxxiii.18, 22, cxix.81, 123 etc.
[2] Isa. xxv.9, xxvi.8, xxx.15, li.5; Jer. xxix.11, xxxi.16 f.; Mic. vii.7; Ps. xlvi.2 (EVV 1).

III. HOPE IN RABBINIC JUDAISM

1. *Linguistic evidence*

'Semitic had no strict equivalent for ἐλπίς.'[1] This remark indicates the linguistic situation for late Judaism in Palestine. There exists in fact no word which could be placed beside ἐλπίς as regards form and content. *Tiqwāh* has almost entirely disappeared[2] and the same is true of the rest of the OT words for which ἐλπίς and ἐλπίζειν appear in the LXX (cf. pp. 8 f). This is all the more striking, since it can by no means be said of the rabbinate that the concept of hope was alien to it. For this body in particular directed its thought very searchingly to the future; proof of this is already afforded by the mere existence of the Apocalypse of Baruch and of IV Ezra, which originated fairly certainly in the circles of the scribes in Palestine. Above all the messianic expectation occupied Palestinian Jewry and their leaders to an extraordinary extent during the first as well as during the second century of our era. In view of this attitude towards the future there must be special reasons for this lack of a word or a phrase defining it as a concept. These reasons can be found only in the particular nature of the future expectation of late rabbinic Judaism. Thus the recognition of the fact that an equivalent for ἐλπίς, ἐλπίζειν is lacking obliges us to analyse the content of the rabbinic expectation of the

[1] Schlatter, *Matt.*, p. 402.
[2] One of the exceptions is in Syr. Bar. lxxviii.6 where *tiqwat 'ōlām, eternal hope*, perhaps occurred in the Hebrew original (Wichmann, p. 39, n. 20).

14

future with a view to finding in it the explanation of the remarkable linguistic state of affairs.

2. *The messianic expectation*

(*a*) The messianic expectation for the future has a positive and a negative aspect. The positive aspect concerns the fulfilment of the hopes of Jewry; the negative one concerns the expectation of judgement which will come upon the ungodly at the dawn of the messianic age. For the latter, being enemies of God, are always also enemies of his people, and conversely by fighting against Jewry they incur the wrath and vengeance of its God. The two aspects of this expectation are intimately linked together, so that they can never be thought of separately, but always only in conjunction. In this context it is of no importance in what order the individual interventions connected with the dawn of the messianic era were expected and to what extent the group of conceptions was elaborated and constantly enlarged, especially with the help of the exegesis of scriptural passages.[1] The extensive complex of premonitory signs of the beginning of the messianic kingdom can also be left out of account here.[2] One point alone is of consequence, namely the fact that the messianic expectation is not a matter for the individual, but for the whole Jewish people and religious community. The individual has a share in it only in so far as he is a member and a part of this community; for the promises according to which the future will belong to God are given to Israel as a whole, and not to Israel as a collection of individual Israelites. Therefore only

[1] cf. the rabbinic material in Strack-Billerbeck, IV, pp. 857 ff.
[2] cf. Str-B. IV, pp. 977 ff.

that non-Jew can become a participant in the blessings
of the promises who has let himself be admitted by
circumcision[1] into the community of the Jewish people
and their religion as a member possessing full rights and
subject to full obligations.[2] But faith in the God of
Jewry does not by itself suffice for this[3]; on the contrary
it must be combined with the fulfilment of all the regu-
lations of the law as well. Amongst these the rule of
circumcision is not indeed put formally into the first
place, but yet from its nature it comes about that its
fulfilment is made to be the prerequisite of all other
real observance of the law.[4]

[1] For circumcision as the prerequisite of messianic salvation see
Str-B. IV, p. 40; as the reason for Israel's deliverance from Gehenna
see Str-B. III, p. 264, IV, pp. 1064 ff.

[2] The σεβόμενοι τὸν θεόν who are frequently mentioned in the
NT undertake only certain obligations (Sabbath, food rules), but
receive no rights, as is shown particularly by their relationship to
the temple and the sacrifices; here they are on exactly the same
legal footing as the pagans (Str-B. II, pp. 548 ff.). The rabbinate
seems all along to have been interested in the σεβόμενοι τὸν θεόν
only in so far as this 'status' contained the possibility of a gradual
transition to Judaism (cf. Juv. 14.96 ff. and the attitude of the
[Pharisaic: Str-B. I, p. 926] merchant Eleazar towards king Izates
of Adiabene: Jos. Ant. 20.17, 34 ff., especially 43 ff.).

[3] cf. for this simply the words of Eleazar to Izates (Jos. Ant.
20.44 ff.): for thou oughtest not only to read them (the Mosaic laws),
but chiefly to practise what they enjoin thee. How long wilt thou continue
uncircumcised? but if thou hast not yet read the law about circumcision, and
dost not know how great impiety thou art guilty of by neglecting it, read
it now.

[4] cf. Str-B. IV, p. 23. The comparatively rare mention in
rabbinic literature of the σεβόμενοι τὸν θεόν (Str-B. II, pp. 716,
719) may be in part at any rate connected with the fact that as the
actual piety of the law increased after the cessation of the cult due
to the destruction of the temple, Judaism came to reject more and
more a merely partial association, such as characterised this group.
The Jew who observes the law faithfully demands complete de-

Now the law is the determining factor for the relationship of the people to God. In it the Jews possess the unmistakable and complete revelation of the divine will. The work of the rabbis serves merely to elucidate it down to its smallest details and to work out all its refinements in order to enable Jewry to carry it out correctly in every particular. For God imparted his will to his people in order that it might be observed, but not in order to provide a consistent view of the world.[1] Since God's will does not change, just because it is God's will, and, moreover, because it is his will, it is always a will to save, the Judaism of the law expects that the coming age will have this in common with the present one, that above them both the law stands as the expression of the divine will. The difference between the two ages consists merely in the fact that the law is now entrusted to Jewry alone, whilst in the coming age the Gentiles too will observe it. This is an idea which occupied a large place, particularly in Hellenistic Jewry, and even determined its missionary work to a large extent[2]; but it was not alien to Palestinian Jewry. This is clear from their expectation that the messiah would teach the nations the law and make them subject to it.[3]

---

votion to it; and so long as this does not exist, he speaks of ἀσέβεια however great may be the leaning towards Judaism, and even if proofs of this are not lacking (cf. p. 16, n. 3).

[1] The rule that the study of the law is to be placed above its observance was first formulated in connexion with the persecution of Hadrian and the increasing difficulties imposed on religious practices by the edicts of the Roman government which was hostile to the law. For further details see Str-B. III, pp. 85 ff.; W. Bacher, *Die Agada der Tannaiten* I (1884), p. 303.

[2] Str-B. III, pp. 98 ff.

[3] cf. especially the Targum on Isa. liii.11, in which the *many* whom the messiah will subject to the law can only be non-Jewish

At the same time it is taken for granted that the messiah will expound the *torah* as no one else has done and that he will leave no doubt about its meaning, in so far as it is obscure or has been explained incorrectly till now.[1] It is also taken for granted that he will observe the *torah* in all its parts,[2] just as God himself also studies the law and keeps its precepts.[3] Since the observance of the law and the messianic expectation are thus bound up together, it is also natural to find that the rabbinate has made the dawn of the messianic era actually to depend on the perfect observance of the law by Israel. Thus according to a saying of R. Simon ben Jochai (c. A.D. 150) the salvation of Israel will begin as soon as the Israelites shall have kept the sabbath properly during the course of two sabbaths (B. Shab. 118b).

(*b*) This leads on to another fundamental factor in the messianic expectation. Its fulfilment does indeed lie in God's hand; but at the same time He has made it depend on the relationship of his people to Himself and to His will. This means that the dawn of the messianic era and of the messianic salvation is not merely God's doing. Man has a share in it and in fact in a

nations. The passages in Str-B. IV, p. 918 also assume that in the age to come the messiah will be actively engaged in teaching which is intended for all mankind. In so far as a difference exists between the expectation of Hellenistic and rabbinic Jewry, it lies only in the fact that the rabbinate, being conscious of its election, restricted its work in the main to the chosen people and attempted to prepare them here for the time of fulfilment.

[1] Str-B. IV, p. 1. Jesus links up with this conception of the new '*torah* of the messiah' by his exposition of the law in the sermon on the mount (Str-B. IV, pp. 1 ff.). Cf. also W. D. Davies, *Torah in the Messianic Age and the Age to Come* (JBL Monograph Series VII, 1952).

[2] Str-B. III, pp. 570 f.

[3] cf. Str-B. IV, pp. 1238 f. Cf. Index under 'God'.

quite decisive manner, namely in so far as it depends on his achievements when the Christ will come and bring in his kingdom. Thus the arrival of the messiah can be hastened, just as it can be delayed.[1] But thereby the messianic expectation of the rabbinate is subject to the same curse of uncertainty which afflicts the expectation of the future in every religion based on achievement. However certain a man may be that fulfilment will come one day, he is depressed by the knowledge that he is perhaps directly guilty of its delay, and it makes no difference whether it is to a greater or smaller extent. For after all there is no human yard-stick by which he might measure how far or how near he is to the goal. It is for God alone to decide this matter and His verdict lies in impenetrable darkness. This alone is certain, that God is absolutely just and that He will make no allowances for the people. In spite of all the ardour in the descriptions of what is to come, this introduces a certain element of weariness and particularly of uncertainty in the rabbinate's expectation of the end. This has been expressed in two ways—in the theory that the messiah is hidden, according to which he is already in existence and is only waiting for the moment of his coming forward,[2] and secondly in the endeavours to calculate in some way the hour of his appearance.[3] In both cases the attempt is made to overcome the uncertainty which arises from attaching the arrival of the messiah to the observance of the law by means of reducing the tension between this uncertainty and God's fixed plan. This has been proved to be the wrong way

[1] cf. for this the passages in Str-B. I, pp. 599 ff.
[2] cf. e.g. Str-B. III, p. 315.
[3] Str-B. IV, pp. 986 ff.

in both cases, since in each the human *ratio* forced its
way into the foreground.

There is no more harrowing testimony to the correct-
ness of this statement than that of Akiba who greeted
Bar-cocheba as the Christ and thereby brought about
the ruin of himself, of most of his pupils and to a large
extent no doubt also of his people.[1] We possess a detailed account of his end at the hands of the Roman
executioners (B. Ber. 61b). According to this he died
with the words confessing the one God of the Jews
(Deut. vi.4) on his lips; consequently he saw nothing
discordant in placing his confession of God and his
confession of Bar-cocheba side by side; on the contrary
this action seemed to him to crown a life dedicated to
God. It can be assumed that Bar-cocheba was still alive
when Akiba died.[2] It is all the more impressive that in
the hour of his death he was concerned only with his
personal relationship to God, and not with the fate of
the movement which by his share in it had brought
about his condemnation to death. The text contains
no suggestion that he had wavered. And yet his last
words as recorded by it convey the impression almost
of a self-justification before God; the speaker is dying
for the sake of God in the service of his law, and not in
service to the messiah. This reveals in a flash, as it were
out of the subconscious, the uncertainty of the messianic
expectation of the rabbinate. This appears also equally
clearly in the fact that no rabbinic saying exists rejecting
as presumptuous and mistaken Bar-cocheba's claim to
be king, not even from the period long after he had

[1] cf. on this A. Schlatter, *Die Tage Trajans und Hadrians* (1897),
pp. 50 ff.
[2] A. Schlatter, *op. cit.*, p. 52.

suffered a terrible end and had dragged Palestinian Jewry with him into destruction.[1] Although this fact implies in part a self-accusation by the rabbinate, yet it also reveals definitely how shaky the ground of the messianic expectation really was, even for those who in this matter had to appear as experts and were considered as such by themselves and by the people.

(c) But the attitude which all this demonstrates is something different from that which is meant by 'hope', even if the Greek word ἐλπίς is disregarded. Here it is always somehow a matter of calculation, made indeed from the human point of view, and it is by this means that the attempt is made to safeguard the expectation. This indicates the suppression of divine sovereignty in the sphere of the messianic hope, even if only in theory. It is therefore only appropriate that the NT should describe the pious Jewish circles at the time of Jesus who were gazing longingly into the future as προσδεχόμενοι (Mark xv.43 et passim) and not as ἐλπίζοντες. This word expresses assurance for the future combined with a consciousness of a rightful claim on the future. Even if it cannot be said that man's demands occupy the foreground, yet the emphasis is placed less on God's goodness, out of which future salvation arises and which can be grasped by faith alone, than on the existing promises which bind God to his people and to the fulfilment of its expectation. Here the question is not *how*, but *when*. Therefore the very nature of the rabbinate's messianic expectation made it impossible to conceive that it would take any other course than that of rejecting Jesus and his demand for faith. For the same reason Jesus' resurrection implied for the Jews the can-

[1] A. Schlatter, *op. cit.*, pp. 52 f.

cellation of their expectation and liberation for a hope which is a true hope because it is altogether bound up with God alone, and not with man.

(*d*) It is no doubt due to the special quality of the messianic hope and to the fact that in the last analysis it is no longer hope, that the idea of the *kingdom of heaven* (*malkūt shāmaim*) has to an increasing extent appeared beside it in Judaism. This appears as a particular entity, distinguished by being mainly concerned with the individual and by the possibility of its being realised. The dissociation in thought between the kingdom of the messiah before the end of the world and the kingdom of God at the last day exists in the meantime already in germ and is realised even now in the relationship of the godly man to God (cf. TWNT I, p. 572); it is also presupposed in the rabbinic apocalypses[1] and allusion is made to it by Paul in I Cor. xv.23; but it is based in the last analysis on the desire to overcome the hopelessness of the individual as a part of his people by making him himself the reason which sustains his hope. Thus the emphasis is of necessity laid upon his own achievements. But this means merely altering the formulation of the problem; it does not in fact solve it. Since the whole life of the godly in the present is determined by his view of the future, the assurance of his personal salvation now becomes the problem. Our sources show that here too the rabbinate failed to provide an answer.

3. *The problem of the assurance of salvation*

(*a*) Beside the messianic expectation shared by the

---

[1] cf. A. Schweitzer, *The Mysticism of Paul the Apostle* (1931, 1953), pp. 75 ff.

whole nation there stands the question of what the individual expects in the future. It concerns his portion in the world to come, which will be assigned in accordance with the decision taken by God Himself[1] when He separates the righteous from the ungodly and banishes the latter to Gehenna,[2] but bestows upon the former the joys of the Garden of Eden in the last days.[3] The decision is made by a forensic act. God ascertains on the basis of the law and of a man's achievements in accordance with it, just who can be regarded as righteous and who cannot be so regarded.[4] As the thought of his achievements has determined the life of the godly man in this age, so it also determines his eternal fate in the same way.

But this introduces into the hope of the individual members of the rabbinate the same element of uncertainty brought out in the analysis of the messianic hope as its most prominent characteristic. It is inherent in every religion based on achievement that its followers cannot reach any assurance whether or not they have obtained the required standard of pious achievement, since they are not acquainted with the rule to which they are subject.[5] This becomes evident in a particularly impressive way in the tenets of rabbinic Judaism, as one of the religions based on achievement, indeed as the classical one. Side by side with the assurance that God is keeping in readiness for the godly all the joys at His command, there stands the uncertainty whether a

---

[1] Str-B. IV, pp. 1100 ff.
[2] Str-B. IV, pp. 1106 f.
[3] Str-B. IV, pp. 1107 f.
[4] cf. e.g. J. AZ 2a, 14 ff. (Str-B. IV, p. 1203).
[5] B. Kid. 40a Bar. (Str-B. II, p. 427).

man's own achievement will after all suffice for him to receive the blessing of salvation with the godly[1] and whether it will not perhaps turn out in the end that God's legal claim can simply never be fully met. This lack of assurance of personal salvation[2] threw deep shadows on the last hours of more than one of the great teachers of Jewry. Rabban Johanan ben Zakkai, the contemporary of the apostles,[3] wept when his disciples approached his sick-bed to receive the last blessing of their dying master; when they asked why he wept he replied: 'Two paths are before me, the one leading to the Garden of Eden, the other to Gehenna, and I do not know along which path they[4] are taking me—why then should I not weep?' (B. Ber. 28b). This is said by the same man whom his disciples have just called 'the shining light of Israel' and 'the strong hammer'. It was the same in the case of R. Johanan (ben Nappacha) (died c. A.D. 290), the Palestinian Amora ('interpreter'), in whose academy the Jerusalem Talmud originated. When he was dying he begged to be buried neither in white[5] nor in black garments, but in garments dyed a shimmering colour, so as to be neither white nor black; then if he was given his place amongst the righteous he would not have to be ashamed, and if he was placed

[1] Hence too the warning of Hillel: Do not rely on yourself even up to the day of your death (Ab. 2.4).

[2] This is a characteristic of the whole of rabbinic Judaism (cf. the passages in Str-B. III, pp. 218 ff.).

[3] A. Schlatter, *Jochanan ben Zakkai, der Zeitgenosse der Apostel* (1899).

[4] The plural covers a guarded way of speaking about God, as does also e.g. the δώσουσιν of Luke vi.38 (cf. Dalman, *Worte Jesu* I, p. 183 f.).

[5] The rabbis, like the NT, considered the garments of the righteous to be white.

amongst the sinners ($r^e sh\bar{a}'\bar{i}m$) he would not be shamed[1]
(J. Kil. 32b, 8 ff.).[2] In both cases the lack of assurance
remains final. 'A confidence based on works does not
ensure certainty and fear gains the victory over faith.'[3]
It makes no real difference to this state of affairs that
we also possess accounts of rabbis who when dying felt
confident about their future.[4] The basic mood of the
rabbinate when considering the judgement is pessi-
mistic,[5] and this mood finds its classic expression in the
constantly continuing casuistical discussions. There is
perhaps no more striking illustration than the story that
the schools of Hillel and Shammai had disputed for
more than two years whether it would be better for
man not to have been created, or whether it was good
for him to have been created; and that they had agreed
upon the conclusion that it would be better for him
not to have been created (B. Erub. 13b Bar.). Indeed
no other attitude is possible 'under the law'.

The fact that within the sphere of nomism no uni-
versal hope exists[6] has been expressed by no one more

[1] The statement presupposes the view that man 'comes back'
as he 'goes'; this view had been generally accepted.

[2] cf. also Gn. r. 96.5 on xlvii.29; and 100.1 on xlix.33.

[3] A. Schlatter, *op. cit.*, p. 73 on the death of Johanan ben Zakkai.

[4] cf. the two accounts in Gn. r. 100.1 on xlix.33 and parallels.

[5] In addition cf. the fact that it was Akiba who frequently
quoted Ecclesiastes with approval: see *Jew. Enc.* I, p. 305.

[6] In connexion with this statement it is interesting to note that
Akiba used the description of God as *miqwēh yisrā'ēl* (*hope of Israel*)
in Jer. xvii.13 in the sense of an *immersion-pool*: Yoma 8.9: 'And it
is said: *miqweh yisrā'ēl* is Yahweh. What is meant by the *miqweh*?
It cleanses the unclean. Thus does the Holy One, praised be He,
also cleanse Israel.' At the same time in the context in question
the literal meaning of this formula would have been most suitable.
[Note: *miqwāh* occurs in Isa. xxii.11 in the sense of *reservoir*, from a
root meaning 'to collect'.]

clearly than by the Johannine Jesus (John v.45): ἔστιν ὁ κατηγορῶν ὑμῶν Μωϋσῆς, εἰς ὃν ὑμεῖς ἠλπίκατε. Here the absurdity of hope on the basis of the religion of the law is stated with the utmost trenchancy: he who depends on man for his eternal future will always remain the defendant in the sight of God; and if anyone wants to procure his salvation himself by means of the law, then no one less than Moses himself will accuse him, because he has not understood that in Moses' view God alone leads man to his goal and that God alone gives him the credit which preserves him from destruction (cf. John v.44).

(b) The rabbinate with full awareness of its position took various paths in order to overcome its lack of assurance of salvation. Thus Akiba advocated the thesis that man becomes sure of God's favour in prayer.[1] Akin to this[2] is the effort to draw conclusions about his eternal fate from the manner of a man's dying.[3] The most vigorous attempt at abolishing the agonising uncertainty is however the so-called 'theology of suffering'.[4] This[5] undertakes to interpret the suffering which befalls the godly; and it does so in fact particularly by explaining it as the discipline which gives him the

[1] T. Ber. 3.3.

[2] Akiba's thesis is closely related to that of the famous man of prayer, Choni, who recognised that his prayer was acceptable when it was 'fluent', i.e. when he could pray without faltering (B. Ber. 34b Bar.).

[3] cf. the catalogue in B. Ket. 103b, and also the passages in Wichmann, p. 3, n. 4.

[4] The name goes back to the phrase 'Theology of suffering' ('Theologie des Leidens'), coined by P. Volz in *Jüdische Eschatologie von Daniel bis Akiba* (1903), p. 155.

[5] Evidence for this exists also outside the rabbinate, but here it was most widespread (Wichmann, p. 51).

possibility already in this life of paying the penalty for his guilt for which he would otherwise have had to atone completely after his death.[1] Here the wish predominates to reduce the unknown number of lapses and thus to give an increasing preponderance to a man's merits, with the result that the just God will not be able to help acquitting him and admitting him into the Garden of Eden, this being of course only what God wishes to do.[2] It is significant that this doctrine was most lastingly defined and developed by Akiba and his school.[3] According to the tradition[4] he smiled as he stood at the death-bed of his teacher, Eliezer ben Hyrcanus, writhing in pain, and explained his smile by saying that he was glad of these pains, because he saw in them a guarantee that God was mercifully disposed towards his teacher. Perhaps this lay also at the root of his own attitude during his martyrdom, and of that particular feature of it which made it appear as the expression of self-justification before God (cf. p. 20). It must be admitted that this attempt of the rabbinate at overcoming their hopelessness also faded into the background again comparatively quickly. Its latest advocate is as early as Rabba ben Joseph ben Chama, a

[1] This must not be confused with the idea of a retribution already in this life; this idea is never found within the framework of the 'theology of suffering' (Wichmann, p. 11).

[2] This whole way of looking at the matter is based on the conviction of God's absolute justice (cf. above, pp. 22 f.). God as the Just One gives the godly man by his suffering the opportunity to atone for unknown trespasses in order not to be obliged to reject him. Since God alone has the power to decide who is to participate in atoning suffering, this doctrine actually acquires a predestinarian character.

[3] Wichmann, pp. 56 ff.

[4] B. Sanh. 101a; cf. on this Wichmann, pp. 62f.

Babylonian Amora, at the beginning of the fourth century.[1] The theory failed in the long run because, although it could explain the suffering of the godly, it could not give to their good fortune also a meaning based on God.[2] Thus the theory broke down as a result of its own anthropocentrism. Hence we can recognise once again the point at which the hopelessness of the rabbinate is to be found, namely that it never got away from itself. For hope is possible only when a man has learned that he can contribute nothing to his own salvation, but that God does everything and that it is God's purpose to lead man to this salvation not by way of his achievement, but by granting it to him *sola gratia*.

[1] Wichmann, p. 78.
[2] Wichmann, pp. 77 f.

IV. THE HOPE OF HELLENISTIC JUDAISM

1. *General usage*

Hellenistic Judaism too was of course aware that hope belongs to life (Ecclus. xiv.2) and is destroyed only by death (Ps. Sol. xvii.2). The sick man hopes for recovery (II Macc. ix.22). One man inspires hopes in another (Ecclus. xiii.6). Those who are parted hope (or hope no longer) to see each other again (Tob. x.7).[1] It is true that *A man of no understanding has vain and false hopes* (Ecclus. xxxiv.1: a free rendering of the Hebrew). The hope of the ungodly is vain (Wisd. iii.1; cf. v.14, xvi.29) or uncertain (II Macc. vii.34); if they die they have no ἐλπίς (Wisd. iii.18). The ἐλπίδες of idol-worshippers are set on dead things (Wisd. xiii.10; cf. xv.6, 10) and it is useless to place one's hope on military power (Judith ix.7). But the ἐλπίς of the godly is fixed on God, their saviour.[2] They have good hopes (Letter of Aristeas 261), so they have nothing to fear (Ecclus. xxxiv.16; I Macc. ii.61 f.); for their hope is united with the fear of God (Ecclus. xxxiv.14 f.; Ps. Sol. vi.8; similarly also of the Messiah in Ps. Sol. xvii.44). God is indeed the *hope of all who continue in his ways* (Test. Jud. xxvi.1). Ἐλπίς possesses the quality of confidence (Ecclus. xlix.10; Judith xiii.19; II Macc. xv.7: *trusting with all hope*). The hope of the mighty rests in God (Ps. Sol. xvii.38), but He is above all the *hope of the needy and the poor* (Ps. Sol. v.13, xv.2, xviii.3 *et passim*). Whilst in

---

[1] A variant reading is πιστεύειν. Cf. *Faith* in this series.

[2] Ecclus. xxxiv.13 f.; Ps. Sol. xvii.3; cf. v.16, viii.37, ix.19, xv.1; Susanna 60; Test. Asher vii.7 (variant reading).

these cases the object of hope is usually God's protection and help in general,[1] it can naturally also be help in a particular situation of need (II Macc. xv.7; Judith viii.20; Letter of Aristeas 18: μεγάλη ἐλπίς; Jos. Ant. 12.300: *their hopes of victory in God*).[2] Hope can spring up in the hour of death (II Macc. ix.20). Such hope is denied to the ungodly (Wisd. iii.18; cf. xv.10), but the hope of the godly is *full of immortality* (Wisd. iii.4); it is directed towards the resurrection (II Macc. vii.11, 14, 20), it is the *hope of salvation from God* (IV Macc. xi.7). Beside this there is the lively eschatological hope of the restoration of Israel (II Macc. ii.18; Test. Benjamin x.11), or of the time of salvation; the evidence for this is supplied by the rabbinic, and especially by the apocalyptic literature.[3]

2. *Philo*

In Philo Greek psychology makes itself felt, in so far as for him ἐλπίς is essentially *expectation* (*Leg. All.* II.43)[4]; nevertheless he also uses the word ἐλπίς in accordance

[1] Here too it can be said that God is the ἐλπίς (cf. p. 11, n. 4); cf. the Greek translation of Ps. xiv.6, xxii.9; in addition Ecclus. xxxiv.16; Ps. Sol. v.13, xv.2.

[2] Josephus generally observes the Greek linguistic usage. Thus for him ἐλπίς also means the expectation of something evil: *Ant.* 2.211, 6.215, 11.247. It is the expectation of something desirable in *Ant.* 17.1; in *Bell.* 6.264, 383. Thus the frequent Greek phrase παρ' ἐλπίδα(ς) in *Ant.* 7.179, 198 *et passim* (also κατ' ἐλπίδα in *Ant.* 16.322). Ἐλπὶς σωτηρίας as in Greek in *Ant.* 16.389; *Bell.* 7.165, 331; ἐλπὶς βεβαία (sure) in *Bell.* 7.413; *Ant.* 8.280. Whilst Jos. *Ant.* 8.282, 12.300 uses the OT phrase 'to have hopes in God' in *Bell.* 2.391, 6.99 he says: '(God) *whom you looked to as ally*'.

[3] Bousset-Gressmann, pp. 202 ff.; Pott, *op. cit.*, pp. 10 ff. According to Ethiopic Enoch xl.9 there is an angel *who is set over the penitence and hope of those who inherit eternal life*.

[4] Ἐλπίζειν =to await in *Leg. All.* III.87; *Cher.* 75; *Det. Pot. Ins.* 160; *Fug.* 164 *et passim*.

with later Greek usage ordinarily for the expectation of good (*Abr.* 14). Thus he considers ἐλπίς and χαρά (*joy*) to be similar (*Det. Pot. Ins.* 140) and he is particularly fond of describing ἐλπίς (as contrasted with φόβος (*fear*) in *Abr.* 14; *Mut. Nom.* 163) as the pleasure of anticipation.[1] As in Greek ἐλπίς corresponds in his view to μνήμη (*memory*); it is also in accordance with Greek[2] thought to consider ἐλπίς as a comfort in trouble (*Jos.* 20.144); for in all cases hope is here directed to a picture of the future planned by men: without such a hope life is not worth living (*Praem. Poen.* 72).

However, where Philo deals with hope particularly, he is not concerned with ideas of the future which display human and earthly desires; the object of ἐλπίς is rather that man should attain perfection (*Rer. Div. Her.* 311); and in this sense ἐλπίς is one of the qualities of the one who is truly a man, of the rational nature (*Det. Pot. Ins.* 138 f.). He who does not 'hope in God' is not a proper man; Philo exemplifies this several times by Enoch ('Ενώς = ἄνθρωπος), who according to Gen. iv.26 was the first to hope in God.[3] Enoch is the *one who always desired the excellent but has not yet been able to attain to it* (*Abr.* 47). 'Ελπίς should be directed towards God, whilst the body is concerned with desire (*Poster. C.* 26). Yet Philo can also speak more generally in the OT sense of the hope which addresses itself to God as saviour (*Leg. Gai.* 196), who bestows gifts contrary to

---

[1] *Leg. All.* III.86 f.; *Mut. Nom.* 161-5; *Exsecr.* 180. Thus he also not infrequently uses εὔελπις and εὐελπιστία, see Leisegang, *Index* (1926).

[2] *Leg. All.* II.42 f. where it is joined by αἴσθησις (*perception*) as a third term (cf. p. 1); in *Migr. Abr.* 154 the *expectation of things to come* appears as a third term.

[3] *Det. Pot. Ins.* 138 f.; *Abr.* 7-14; *Praem. Poen.* 11-14.

and beyond what is hoped for,[1] to God's gracious nature (*Spec. Leg.* I.310, II.196) or to the gentleness of His nature (*Fug.* 99), the hope in particular which expects forgiveness (*Fug.* 99; *Spec. Leg.* II.196). This hope is intimately connected with πίστις (*Leg. All.* III.164). The ἐλπίδες of the wicked are certainly not fulfilled (*Exsecr.* 142, 149; cf. *Praem. Poen.* 12[2]). Eschatological hopes play no part in Philo, but Moses has *the hope of coming immortality* (*Virt.* 67).

[1] *Leg. All.* III.85; *Sacr. A.C.* 78; *Somn.* I.71; *Decal.* 16; *Spec. Leg.* II.219; cf. also H. Windisch, *Die Frömmigkeit Philos* (1909), pp. 53 ff.)

[2] Unfulfilled hopes are mentioned elsewhere too, e.g. *Epigr. Graec.* 497.5: the unfulfilled hopes of parents whose daughter has died.

V. THE EARLY CHRISTIAN
CONCEPT OF HOPE

1. *General usage*

The concept of hope in the NT is determined in its essentials by that of the OT.[1] Only when hope in the profane sense is in question does the element of expectation, a characteristic of the Greek ἐλπίζειν, usually predominate. Yet the word ἐλπίζειν is always used only when something acceptable is expected and the differentiation between ἀγαθή and πονηρὰ ἐλπίς is lacking.

Thus ἐλπίζειν (ἐλπίς) in the profane sense means 'to expect' with a hint of 'to reckon on' in Luke vi.34; I Cor. ix.10; II Cor. viii.5; I Tim. iii.14; Acts xvi.19; Herm. v. III.11.3. There is no doubt a stronger emphasis on 'hoping' in Luke xxiii.8; Acts xxiv.26, xxvii.20; this is more evident still in Luke xxiv.21; Rom. xv.24; I Cor. xvi.7; Phil. ii.19, 23; Philemon 22; II John 12; III John 14; Ign. Eph. i.2, x.1; Rom. i.1; Barn. xvii.1. But when such expectation refers to the behaviour of people, the confidence, characteristic of the OT concept, comes to the fore: II Cor. i.13, v.11, xiii.6 and especially II Cor. i.7, x.15, as the interchange with the

[1] For grammatical questions cf. the grammars. ʼΕλπίζειν is employed as in the LXX with its object denoted by ἐπί with the dative or accusative or by ἐν or εἰς (cf. p. 11, n. 3). The dative alone is used once: Matt. xii.21. ʼΕλπίς can denote not only the attitude of hopefulness, but also rhetorically the thing hoped for (Rom. viii.24; Col. i.5; Titus ii.13; Heb. vi.18; in the LXX II Macc. vii.14); this is also a common Greek usage (e.g. Aesch. *Choeph.* 778; cf. p. 6, n. 5, and for the alternation of ἐλπίς and ἔλπισμα cf. Plut. *Suav. Viv. Epic.* 6 (II.1090 d), cf. p. 4, n. 3. The concept of hope is not modified by this usage.

idea of πεποίθησις shows; for this word in i.15 refers back
to ἐλπίζειν (verse 13) and takes the place of ἐλπίς in
viii.22, x.2 (cf. e.g. i.7, x.15). In I Cor. xiii.7 hope, like
love, clearly has a person as its object, although this
attitude is based for Paul too on the corresponding
attitude towards God, as the natural transition from
the one to the other indicates. And the insertion of
πάντα ἐλπίζει, fitted in between πάντα πιστεύει and πάντα
ὑπομένει, demonstrates that the three verbs describe an
attitude which is all of one piece.

2. The nature of hope

If hope is fixed on God, it comprises just these three
elements combined in one: expectation of what is to
come, confidence and patience in waiting; and first one
and then another can be emphasised or explicitly
brought into relief. The definition of πίστις in Heb. xi.1
as ἐλπιζομένων ὑπόστασις corresponds fully to the OT
idea that πιστεύειν and ἐλπίζειν belong together (Ps.
lxxviii.22) and the usage of the LXX which renders
tiqwāh (Ezek. xix.5; Ruth i.12) and tōḥelet (Ps. xxxviii.7
[EVV 8]) with ὑπόστασις[1] beside ἐλπίς (p. 9). It is
emphasised that the confidence placed in the future
bestowed by God can be trusted,[2] and the added phrase
ἔλεγχος[3] πραγμάτων οὐ βλεπομένων lays still further stress
on the paradoxical nature of this hopeful confidence,
in so far as it simply cannot reckon on what is under

[1] ‘Υποστῆναι appears for yḥl (p. 9) in Micah v.7 (Heb. 6); so
too for ḥsh (p. 9) in Judges ix.15.
[2] cf. in the following verses particularly, verse 10: ἧς τεχνίτης . . .
θεός; verse 11: ἐπεὶ πιστὸν ἡγήσατο τὸν ἐπαγγειλάμενον; verse 19:
λογισάμενος ὅτι . . .; verse 23: οὐκ ἐφοβήθησαν . . .; verse 27:
μὴ φοβηθεὶς κτλ.
[3] This word is used in the LXX mainly for tokaḥat (proof).

man's control.[1] It is just this element in ἐλπίς which
Paul too brings out in his 'definition' in Rom. viii.24 f.:
ἐλπὶς δὲ βλεπομένη οὐκ ἔστιν ἐλπίς· ὃ γὰρ βλέπει τις, τί καὶ
ἐλπίζει; In this question there is first of all an argument
of formal logic (suitable to the context), which states
that hope, as an attitude directed to the future, can
only after all be spoken of when its object is not actually
present. Yet in Paul's view its positive meaning lies in
the fact that ἐλπίς cannot be directed to βλεπόμενα because these are πρόσκαιρα (II Cor. iv.18); for whatever
is seen belongs surely to the sphere of *flesh* (σάρξ[2]), on
which no hope can be based. But Paul goes on to lay
stress on the element of patient waiting which also belongs to ἐλπίς (on I Cor. xiii.7 cf. p. 34) when he con-
tinues: εἰ δὲ ὃ οὐ βλέπομεν ἐλπίζομεν, δι' ὑπομονῆς
ἀπεκδεχόμεθα. This quality in ἐλπίς permits him to
employ also the paradox in Rom. iv.18: ὃς παρ' ἐλπίδα
ἐπ' ἐλπίδι ἐπίστευσεν; when the limit of reckoning with
what is under our own control had been reached, then
confidence in God's future stepped in. The element of
firm confidence also determines the meaning of ἐλπίζειν
in I Cor. xv.19; II Cor. i.10, iii.12; Phil. i.20; Heb.
iii.6; I Peter i.21: ὥστε τὴν πίστιν ὑμῶν καὶ ἐλπίδα εἶναι
εἰς θεόν,[3] whilst the idea of patient waiting receives the

[1] cf. again in the following verses, verse 7: περὶ τῶν μηδέπω
βλεπομένων; verse 8: μὴ ἐπιστάμενος . . .; verse 19: παραβολῇ
ἐκομίσατο; verse 25: μᾶλλον . . . ἢ πρόσκαιρον ἔχειν . . . ἀπόλαυσιν;
verse 27: τὸν . . . ἀόρατον ὡς ὁρῶν ἐκαρτέρησεν.

[2] cf. TWNT VII. Cf. also J. A. T. Robinson, *The Body* (1952).

[3] It is possible in this passage to take τὴν πίστιν ὑμῶν and (τὴν)
ἐλπίδα as the co-ordinated subject of εἶναι. In that case πίστις and
ἐλπίς together describe that OT concept of confident hope. Alternatively ἐλπίδα can be considered to be the predicate: *so that your
faith is at the same time hope in God.* This affirms that faith includes
confident waiting on God's future.

chief emphasis in Rom. v.4 f., xv.4; I Thess. i.3 (τῆς ὑπομονῆς τῆς ἐλπίδος), v.8 (ἐλπίδα σωτηρίας, cf. Ps. lxxviii.22); Heb. vi.11, x.23. But of course we must not think that either element is ever eliminated.[1]

Whilst in this respect the structure of the ἐλπίς concept does not differ from that of the OT, there is a difference from the OT in the circumstances of the man who hopes, as demonstrated particularly in II Cor. iii.1-18. The πεποίθησις in verse 4 and the ἐλπίς in verse 12 of which Paul boasts no doubt include also his hopeful confidence in the Corinthians (i.13, 15), but they are in a much more fundamental sense the apostolic reliance and certainty which he has as διάκονος of the καινὴ διαθήκη. They have the same meaning as the ἐλευθερία[2] (verse 17) which is freedom from the law, and from death, so that παρρησία (verse 12, vii.4) and καύχησις (i.12, vii.4, x.8 ff., xi.16 ff.) are based on it.[3] Thus Christian ἐλπίς rests on God's act of salvation effected in Christ, and since this is an eschatological act, ἐλπίς itself appears as an eschatological blessing, i.e. now is the time in which one may have confident trust.[4] The waiting, which is part of ἐλπίς, is therefore

[1] Ἐλπίζειν (ἐλπίς) meaning 'trust' occurs also in I Clem. xi.1, xii.7 (combined with πιστεύειν); II Clem. xvii.7; Barn. vi.3; Herm. m. XII.5.2, 6.4; Just. Dial. 35.2. The contrast in John v.45: Μωϋσῆς, εἰς ὃν ὑμεῖς ἠλπίκατε: on whom you base your security (cf. pp. 25 f.); cf. Barn. xvi.1 f.

[2] cf. TWNT II, pp. 492 ff.

[3] cf. with this particularly II Cor. xi.17: ἐν ταύτῃ τῇ ὑποστάσει τῆς καυχήσεως (cf. pp. 8f.) and for the concept of καύχησις (TWNT III pp. 646 ff.) cf. Rom. v.2: καυχώμεθα ἐπ᾽ ἐλπίδι τῆς δόξης τοῦ θεοῦ and Heb. iii.6: τὸ καύχημα τῆς ἐλπίδος. In the LXX ἐλπίς and ὑπόστασις as well as καύχησις are used for tōḥelet (Prov. xi.7), cf. p. 9.

[4] cf. p. 11, n. 3. When Paul quotes Isa. xi.10 in Rom. xv.12 it indicates that in his view that promise is now fulfilled.

itself achieved by the spirit, the gift of the last days[1] and is based on πίστις in the act of salvation (Gal. v.5), just as being in ἐλπίς in Rom. viii.24 f. is then immediately described in verses 26 f. as being assisted by the πνεῦμα.

Thus ἐλπίς together with πίστις makes up the Christian being. Hence the expression of blessing in Rom. xv.13; hence the characteristic quality of the Christians is that they are τῇ ἐλπίδι χαίροντες in Rom. xii.12, and hence that of the pagans is μὴ ἔχοντες ἐλπίδα in I Thess. iv.13,[2] which of course does not mean that they do not make for themselves any pictures of a future after death, but that they can have no well-founded confidence in the future. In so far as πίστις is active in ἀγάπη[3] (Gal. v.6), πίστις, ἀγάπη and ἐλπίς make up the Christian being, as Paul describes it in I Thess. i.3, and as he sets out its qualities in I Cor. xiii.13, no doubt as an antithesis to a Gnostic formula.[4] The basic OT concept of hope also enables us to understand why Paul can say that ἐλπίς too remains, even though one day βλέπειν will be achieved (I Cor. xiii.12); for ἐλπίς is not directed towards realising a picture of the future as projected by man, but is the trust in God which turns away from itself and the world, which waits patiently for God's gift, and which, when He has given it, does not consider it to be a possession at one's own disposal, but is confidently assured that God also will maintain what He has bestowed. Christian being—in accordance with its understanding of God—can never be conceived as perfect apart from ἐλπίς. Before it is achieved, emphasis

---

[1] So also Barn. xi.11.

[2] So also in Eph. ii.12 (with the characteristic addition that the pagans are ἄθεοι); II Clem. i.7.

[3] cf. *Love* in this series, esp. p. 59.   [4] cf. p. 6, n. 3.

may be placed on tarrying and patient waiting on the future: Rom. v.2, 4 f., viii.20, 24 f.; I Cor. xv.19; Gal. v.5; I Thess. ii.19, which indeed would not be the case, if in the phrase τῇ γὰρ ἐλπίδι ἐσώθημεν (Rom. viii.24) the word ἐσώθημεν was not stressed and if παρρησία and καύχησις did not spring from it.

3. *The eschatological element*

Apart from Paul, in the NT the concept of ἐλπίς has little place in the Johannine writings (on John v.45 cf. p. 36, n. 1). It appears in them as a hope fixed on future fulfilment only in I John iii.3. But what ἐλπίζειν denotes can in fact be subsumed in the πίστις concept, and so it is in John.[1] That in Revelation ἐλπίς is lacking altogether can astonish only those who overlook the fact that the idea of hope is included here in the ὑπομονή concept.

Elsewhere, especially where Jewish influence is strong, the element of waiting for the eschatological future is very pronounced: Col. i.5; I Tim. iv.10; Titus ii.13, iii.7; I Peter i.3, 13; Heb. vi.18 f., vii.19[2]; in Acts it has one object only, namely the resurrection from the dead: xxiii.6, xxiv.15, xxvi.6 f., xxviii.20; just as, in Acts ii.26, Ps. xvi.9 (EVV 10) is explained as referring to the resurrection of Christ.[3] The paradox that Christian ἐλπίς is itself already an eschatological blessing, because in it the OT hope is known to be fulfilled by the sending of Jesus, is found most clearly in Matt. xii.21, which applies Isa. xlii.4 to Jesus (cf. Rom. xv.12) and in

---

[1] See *Faith* in this series, esp. pp. 97 ff.

[2] With the same meaning in Barn. viii.5; Just. *Dial.* 44.4; Athenag. 33.1; Sib. Or. ii.53.

[3] Ἐλπίς in I Clem. xxvii.1 also has the resurrection in view.

I Peter i.3: (ὁ θεός) ὁ ἀναγεννήσας ἡμᾶς εἰς ἐλπίδα ζῶσαν δι' ἀναστάσεως Ἰησοῦ Χριστοῦ ἐκ νεκρῶν.[1] In a somewhat more conventional manner it is used also in those cases in which Christ himself is designated as our ἐλπίς,[2] in which the ἐλπίς bestowed on us is mentioned[3] and in which ἐλπίς, associated with other concepts[4] or alone[5] appears as the distinctive mark of Christianity. Such phrases are sometimes almost like formulae; this is evident particularly in Barn. i.4, 6, where πίστις is no longer the basis of ἐλπίς, as with Paul, but on the contrary πίστις is resting on ἐλπίς.

The fact that—apart from Revelation—no detailed pictures of the future are sketched shows that the quality of trusting in God's action is preserved as an inherent element of hopeful waiting, and this is occasionally brought out strongly by the way it is formulated.[6] Similarly the quality of patient waiting is sometimes

[1] Ign. Mg. ix.1; Barn. xvi.8.

[2] Col. i.27; I Tim. i.1; Ign. Eph. xxi.2; Mg. xi.1; Tr. Introduction ii.2; Phld. xi.2; cf. p. 11, n. 4, p. 30, n. 1. Hope in Jesus (ἐπὶ or εἰς) in Barn. vi.3, xi.11; Just. Dial. 16.4, 47.2 et passim; in his cross: Barn. xi.8; cf. Just. Dial. 96.1, 110.3; in his name (ὄνομα) in Barn. xvi.8 (I Clem. lix.3: in the name of God: a Jewish feature).   [3] II Thess. ii.16; cf. I Clem. lvii.2.

[4] Col. i.4 f. (ἀκούσαντες τὴν πίστιν ὑμῶν ... καὶ τὴν ἀγάπην ἣν ἔχετε ... διὰ τὴν ἐλπίδα). Titus i.1 f. (ἀπόστολος ... κατὰ πίστιν ἐκλεκτῶν θεοῦ καὶ ἐπίγνωσιν ἀληθείας τῆς κατ' εὐσέβειαν ἐπ' ἐλπίδι ζωῆς αἰωνίου). Heb. x.22-24; Ign. Mg. vii.1; Phld. xi.2; I Clem. lviii.2 (the wording of an oath); Barn. iv.8, xi.8; Just. Dial. 110.3; especially the variations on the triad of 1 Cor. xiii.13; Barn. i.4, i.6; Pol. iii.2 f.

[5] Col. i.23; Eph. i.18, iv.4; especially I Peter iii.15 (... λόγον περὶ τῆς ἐν ὑμῖν ἐλπίδος); I Clem. li.1; Ign. Eph. i.2; Phld. v.2. For the concept: κοινὴ ἐλπίς see Thuc. II.43.6; Lys. 2.9.

[6] I Peter i.3; Titus i.2, ii.13 f., iii.5-7. The fact that ἐλπίς and πίστις belong together appears from the way they are mentioned in Barn. iv.8.

emphasised.[1] The fact that ἐλπίς does not stand by itself
in the Christian life, but develops into a fresh attitude
to the world, is not only expressed in those stereotyped
descriptions of Christian behaviour, but is now and
then explicitly stressed.[2]

[1] Col. i.23; Heb. vi.18 f., x.23. Ign. Phld. v.2; Pol. viii.1;
II Clem. xi.5.

[2] I John iii.3 (πᾶς ὁ ἔχων τὴν ἐλπίδα ταύτην ἐπ' αὐτῷ ἁγνίζει
ἑαυτόν...); Eph. iv.1-4; I Tim. v.5 (a contrast in vi.17); Titus
ii.11-14; I Peter i.13; Ign. Mg. ix.1; Barn. xi.11; Athenag. 33.1.
Herm. says repeatedly that sin causes hope to be lost: v. I.1.9,
m. V.1.7, s. VIII.9.4, IX.14.3, IX.26.2. But for Herm. there is a
fresh hope, the hope of penitence: s. VI.2.4, VIII.6.5, VIII.7.2,
VIII.10.2.

APPENDIX

(a) Ἀπελπίζω is first found in the later Greek literature, in which it is used beside the verbs ἀπογινώσκειν and ἀπονοεῖσθαι, which were common earlier, with the same meaning.[1] The meaning is: *not to believe*, or *hope*, that something will happen; thus generally that of the Latin *desperare* (as well apparently as *desperare facio*)[2]; it takes the accusative and is also used in the passive. Amongst its many possible applications[3] that to illness or, alternatively, to recovery is especially frequent; a sick man who is 'given up' is an ἀπελπισθείς or ἀπηλπισ-μένος.[4]

In the Septuagint ἀπελπίζειν occurs with the general meaning of *giving up hope* in Ecclus. xxii.21, xxvii.21 (both times referring to a friendship in danger) and in II Macc. ix.18 with reference to illness. It is noteworthy that in Isa. xxix.19 *the poor among men* is rendered by ἀπηλπισμένοι τῶν ἀνθρώπων, and its use in Judith ix.11, where God is invoked, agrees with this: *thou art a God of the afflicted, thou art a helper of the oppressed, an*

[1] Attested first in Hyperides 5.35 (p. 88 Jensen). Cf. L. Götzeler, *De Polybi Elocutione* (Diss. Erlangen, 1887), p. 23; P. Linde, *Breslauer philol. Abhandlungen* IX.3 (1906), pp. 31 f.

[2] So evidently in *Anth. Pal.* XI.114.6 and certainly in the patristic literature, see Thes. Steph., s.v.

[3] cf. Polyb. 23.13.2; Andronicus, *De Passionibus*, p. 14, 14 (Kreuttner); Nero in Ditt Syll (ed. 3, p. 814, 10 f.); cf. p. 7.

[4] E.g. Ditt Syll ed. 3, p. 1173, 7.11: further material in O. Weinreich, *Antike Heilungswunder* (1909), pp. 195 f.; K. Kerényi, *Die Griech.-oriental. Romanliteratur* (1927) p. 27, n. 11. Ἀπογινώσκειν is also used in the same sense. This word is not found in the NT, but it is in the LXX and in Herm. (see Pr-Bauer).

*upholder of the weak, a protector of the forlorn, a saviour of
the despairing* (ἀπηλπισμένων).[1]

In the NT ἀπηλπικότες appears in Eph. iv.19 as a
variant reading (D 257 Lat syr^p), in place of ἀπηλγηκότες,
(to *become callous*), as a distinctive mark of pagans; it is
used absolutely, as in Isa. xxix.19 and in Judith ix.11.
God is also described in I Clem. lix.3 as *saviour of* τῶν
ἀπηλπισμένων, as he is in Judith ix.11. Figuratively in
Herm. v. III.12.2 an old man who has lost all hope is
described as ἀφηλπικὼς ἑαυτόν. In the Apologists the
word does not occur.

Its use in Luke vi.35 is unique: δανίζετε μηδὲν
ἀπελπίζοντες. For according to verse 34 (ἐὰν δανίσητε
παρ' ὧν ἐλπίζετε λαβεῖν) it can only be understood as
lend without expecting to be repaid (or if interest were in
mind *without expecting any return*).[2]

Thus ἀπελπίζειν would be used in accordance with
the analogy of ἀπαιτεῖν and similar words (a usage
authenticated only from Chrysostom onwards)[3] or it is
an example of abbreviation (ἀπελπίζω = ἀπολαμβάνειν
ἐλπίζω) and that is how the Vulgate translates it: *nihil
inde sperantes*. The usual meaning of ἀπελπίζειν could only
lead to the translation *where you despair of nothing* (Old
Latin: *nihil desperantes*) which could probably only mean:

---

[1] In Josephus ἀπελπίζειν is often found with the usual meaning
of 'giving up hope', see Schlatter, *Lukas*, p. 249 (on Luke vi.35).
Philo, according to Leisegang's *Index*, does not use ἀπελπίζειν; he
uses ἀπογινώσκειν often with τὰς ἐλπίδας as its object (see Leisegang). This occurs in the LXX only in Deut. xxxiii.9 (for *ignored*);
Judith ix.11 (cf. above); II Macc. ix.22.

[2] In that case there would be a parallel to this saying in a
rabbinic precept handed down several times: 'He . . . who lends
without interest is considered (by God) to have kept all the com-
mandments' (Str-B. II, p. 159).

[3] See Zahn, *Lukas* (1913), *ad loc.*

where you hope for a heavenly compensation.[1] But this suits
the context no better than the sense which, following
the reading μηδένα ἀπελπίζοντες (LA X, syrᵖ etc.) would
yield the meaning: *where you despair of no one, do not give
up hope for anyone* (or if ἀπελπίζειν is taken transitively,
where you bring none to despair). Since the first meaning is linguistically satisfactory, the proposed conjecture
ἀνελπίζοντες, which would give the same meaning, is
unnecessary.

(*b*) Προσελπίζω, *to hope for beforehand,* seems to be
attested only by Posidippus (third century B.C.) in
Athen. IX.20 (377c) apart from Christian literature.

According to Eph. i.12 'we' are chosen by the will
of God: εἰς τὸ εἶναι ἡμᾶς εἰς ἔπαινον δόξης αὐτοῦ, τοὺς
προηλπικότας ἐν τῷ Χριστῷ.[2] If the author includes himself with the Jewish Christians as belonging to a special
group of believers, then he is using the προ- to mean
either *earlier than the Gentiles* or *already before Christ was
sent,* which would fit in well with the thought that
Christ is the fulfilment of the OT hope (cf. pp. 36 f.).
If on the other hand 'we' is understood to mean all
Christians, then προ- is used from the standpoint of the
present with the eschatological fulfilment in view. But
this is probably less likely. The word does not occur
in the Apostolic Fathers nor in the Apologists.

[1] See Klostermann, *Lukas* (²1929), *ad loc.*
[2] For the construction with ἐν, cf. p. 33, n. 1.

INDEX OF REFERENCES

APOCRYPHA AND PSEUDEPIGRAPHA

RABBINIC

(B or J *indicates Babylonian or Jerusalem Talmud. Bar.=Baraitha* (outside) *after a reference indicates a passage not incorporated in the official Mishnah.*)

Talmud and Midrash

EARLY CHRISTIAN WRITINGS

Epistle of Barnabas (Barn.)

I Clement (I Clem.)

II Clement (II Clem.)

Hermas (Herm.) m=Mandates
s=Similitudes
v=Visions

Ignatius (Ign.)
Ephesians (Eph.)

Magnesians (Mg.)

Philadelphians (Phld.)

Trallians (Tr.)

Polycarp (Pol.)

GENERAL INDEX

51